Table of Contents

- **Chapter 1 - The Conditioning of Modern Male Masculinity**
    - 1.1 Early Conditioning
    - 1.2 The Culture of Performance
    - 1.3 Not Toxic Masculinity
    - 1.4 Self-Worth and the Body
    - 1.5 Reclaiming Presence
- **Chapter 2 - Life Contexts**
    - 2.1 Youth & Early Conditioning
    - 2.2 Dating & Single Life
    - 2.3 Marriage & Routine
    - 2.4 Second Life After Divorce
- **Chapter 3— General Guide to Male Pleasure Zones**
- **Chapter 4 - Practices & Rewiring (Self Work)**
    - 4.1 Breath as Anchor
    - 4.2 Conscious Touch (Solo Practice)
    - 4.3 Movement and Stillness
    - 4.4 Ritualized Release and Retention
    - 4.5 Energy Grounding
    - Why This Matters
    - Mirror Work
    - Conscious Self-Practice (Steps)
    - Daily Self-Practice Checklist
- **Chapter 5 - Partner Work**
    - Shifting From Performance to Presence
    - Translating Solo Practice Into Partnered Intimacy
    - Communication as Embodiment
    - Expanding Pleasure Zones Together
    - From Quick Release to Shared Arc
    - The Reward of Presence
    - Guided Partner Flows

Table of Contents

- **Chapter 6 - Why This Works**
    - 6.1 Rewiring Attention & Sensation (Interoception)
    - 6.2 Resetting the Nervous System
    - 6.3 Conditioning & Resensitization
    - 6.4 Pelvic Floor & Circulation
    - 6.5 Presence & Secure Connection
    - How Long Does It Take?
    - Common Roadblocks
    - The Core Principle
    - Integration
- **Chapter 7—The Quick Start Guide**
- **Chapter 8—Closing Reflections**

Preface / Purpose

This book is a guide for men who want to reconnect with their bodies, their energy, and their presence. It is not about performance, conquest, or ego. It is about feeling: deeply, fully, and honestly.

Modern culture pushes men toward external validation through achievement, sexual conquest, or "performance" between the sheets. Beneath all of that noise lies a quiet truth: many men are disconnected from their own sensation, from their worth, and from their body as a source of power.

> **Key Ideas**
> - Modern men are trained for performance, not presence.
> - This book is a field guide for rewiring attention, sensation, and self-worth.

This work is about rewiring and creating new habits and practices that bring men out of their heads and back into their bodies. It is about honoring the male form as sacred, experiencing pleasure without shame, and building confidence not through output but through presence. The purpose of this journey is:

To experience the full sensation of the body rather than drifting into distraction.
- To rewire the mind–body connection so intimacy is no longer about pressure or performance.
- To cultivate calm, confidence, and presence that ripple into every part of life.
- To free sexuality from shame and restore it to its rightful place as a sacred expression of life force.

Preface / Purpose

A Note For Women Reading This

If you are reading this to better understand the men in your life, thank you. The best support you can offer is honest feedback and patience while he builds new habits. Do not coach him in the middle of a practice. Agree on words that signal "slow down" and words that signal "keep going." Your safety matters as much as his growth.

Copyright © 2025 Chris Awalt
All rights reserved.

All content in this book reflects the author's personal experience, perspective, and interpretation. Nothing in this book is intended as medical or clinical advice.

This book is intended for informational and personal development purposes. It does not replace medical, psychological, or therapeutic advice.

No part of this book may be reproduced, stored, or transmitted in any form or by any means without prior written permission from the author, except for brief quotations in critical reviews or scholarly work.

All photographs, artwork, diagrams, and layout elements are original to the author unless otherwise noted.

Printed in the United States of America.

Prologue
WHY I WROTE THIS

I didn't write this book to impress anyone or sound enlightened. I wrote it because I reached a point where success and strength weren't enough. I could deliver, lead, and stay in control, but something was missing: connection. My mind was sharp, but my body was muted. I could get things done, yet I rarely felt present while doing them.

My reset started when I learned to pay attention to simple signals: breath, tension, and where my mind went when I was stressed. Energy work, including Reiki, helped me notice what I usually ignored. Tantric study gave me a structure for attention and choice. Life coaching tools helped me make those changes stick in the real world.

This book is a field guide for men who want practical steps, not flowery words. It is about building presence, steadiness, and sensory integrity through the body. It will not tell you to be perfect. It will show you how to be better. To be a little more in tune. To notice what is true in your body and act from that truth.

If you are here, you already know something needs to change. You do not have to become someone else. You need a process to clear noise, rebuild sensation, and carry that into how you work, love, and lead. That is what follows.

When I reference "Divine Masculine," I am not talking about gender roles or rules. I am talking about qualities you can train in your body and behavior. Divine Masculine is about grounded presence, purpose, structure, and clean action. Divine Feminine is about intuition, creativity, receptivity, and flow.

Everyone has both. Many men are strong in doing but weak in feeling. Many can chase goals but cannot sit in silence or hold steady attention with a partner. This book helps you balance that. The goal is not dominance. The goal is integration.

Why it matters now: most men were never taught how to regulate stress, rebuild sensation, or speak honestly about desire. That gap hurts intimacy, health, and leadership. The tools here close that gap.

Chapter 1

THE CONDITIONING OF MODERN MASCULINITY

"Before you change your life, locate your body"

1.1 Early Conditioning

From the earliest stages of boyhood, as the body starts to change and curiosity kicks in, most young men get mixed messages. There's discovery, the new sensations, curiosity, the first spark of sexuality, but then there's the noise that comes with it. Teasing from friends. Jokes from adults. Moments of embarrassment or outright shaming.

Even when it's "just joking," it still lands. It teaches a boy that this natural part of life is something to hide or laugh at That confusion sticks. Is my body something to be proud of or something to conceal?

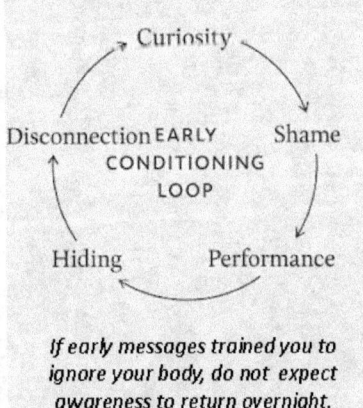

If early messages trained you to ignore your body, do not expect awareness to return overnight. Start small. Name one sensation without judging it

Those early moments become the blueprint for how men later relate to themselves. From the time a boy starts to notice his body, he's collecting data, sometimes from jokes, sometimes from silence, sometimes from shame. A few careless comments about appearance or sexuality can sit in his nervous system for decades, quietly shaping the idea that the male body is something to hide, minimize, or prove.

1.2 The Culture of Performance

As men grow up, the messages don't stop, they just get dressed up differently. Media glorifies stamina, image, dominance. Dating culture rewards conquest. Even long-term relationships can fall into routines where connection gets replaced with counting: how often, how long, how good.

The world keeps repeating the same thing: A man's worth is measured by what he does. Almost never: A man's worth is felt in who he is.

This runs deep. For generations, masculinity has been tied to output and to how much a man can provide, protect, or prove. That mindset built societies, but it also built a lot of disconnection. It taught men to perform instead of feel, to achieve instead of inhabit themselves.

So by the time most men reach adulthood, their sense of worth has been outsourced. The body becomes a tool to test, a machine to maintain, something judged by results instead of honored for simply being alive.

1.3 Not Toxic Masculinity

This book isn't here to glorify "alpha" stereotypes or recycle the cliché of men thinking with their other head. That mindset is part of the problem, educing men to performers, competitors, and conquerors.

Key Ideas
- The body is not a test.
- Reverence ≠ ego.
- Self-worth is built through evidence, not affirmation

What we're doing here is reclaiming the body as sacred, not as a weapon or proof of worth. Real masculinity isn't about domination; it's about integration; head, heart, and body working together.

This isn't about making men softer or weaker. It's about restoring balance. Strength and sensitivity were never opposites. The masculine becomes whole again when he's no longer performing for approval but showing up with grounded presence.

1.4 Self-Worth and the Body

That performance lens blinds men to their own beauty and power. We're taught to see our bodies as practical things that lift, build, work, and protect. Rarely as sacred.

But to appreciate your body, to recognize it as a vessel of energy and design, isn't ego. It's reverence. The male body isn't just an instrument of performance; it's a living system built for clarity, power, and sensation.

When you start to honor it, feed it, breathe into it, listen to it, you rebuild a sense of worth that doesn't depend on anyone's scoreboard. Touching your own body with awareness says, this form is not shameful; it's mine. It's sacred.

1.5 Reclaiming Presence

A lot of men live cut off from their own pleasure. They're numbed by stress, distraction, porn, or the constant grind to perform. Reconnection starts simple: breathe, slow down, notice, receive.

In Reiki we say, energy follows attention. When you focus on the part that hurts and breathe into it, the pain often drops without effort. That's not magic; that's the body finally feeling safe enough to relax.

When a man honors both his physical and energetic body, something shifts. He calms down. His nervous system stops running hot. He can meet his partner without calculation, and himself without judgment. That's presence. That's power

Chapter 2

LIFE CONTEXTS

"Your next chapter starts with your next step."

2.1 Youth & Early Conditioning

Long before a man enters the world of relationships, the patterns that shape how he sees his body and sexuality are already being written. Childhood and adolescence are the soil where seeds of shame, comparison, and performance are planted.

For many boys, the first experiences of sexuality are met not with guidance but with silence, teasing, or punishment. A mother finding a sock under the bed, a peer making jokes in the locker room, or the sting of being compared to others. These small moments accumulate. They create the message: this part of you is embarrassing, and you must either hide it or prove it.

Peer culture compounds the pressure. Boys quickly learn that masculinity is measured by performance: how early you "scored," how many partners you've had, or how impressive your stories sound. The body itself becomes a tool for validation rather than an instrument of connection.

Media and pornography only intensify this confusion. Instead of intimacy, boys learn choreography. Instead of presence, they learn to perform. Instead of feeling, they learn to act. By the time many men reach adulthood, they equate masculinity with conquest, size, and stamina, while having little connection to the sensations and sacredness of their own bodies.

This early conditioning explains why so many men, even in committed relationships, struggle to be fully present. They were trained from the start to live in their heads, anxious about how they measure up, instead of in their bodies, attuned to what they feel.

Rewiring begins by stripping away years of learned shame and performance-based thinking. It is remembering what was always true: the body is not a joke, not a burden, not an embarrassment. It is a vessel of life force designed to feel deeply, to connect authentically, and to create not just children, but   intimacy, vitality, and power. When men reclaim this truth, the cycle of teasing, shame, and comparison loses its hold. Presence replaces performance, appreciation replaces embarrassment, and self-respect becomes the foundation upon which all intimacy is built.

2.2 Dating & Single Life
For the single man, modern dating can feel like a minefield. On the surface it promises freedom and variety, but beneath that freedom often lies a subtle emptiness. Dating apps reduce connection to swipes and photos. Conversations become performance. Sex can be easy to find yet carry little depth.

In this environment, men are conditioned to approach intimacy as transactional: win her attention, prove your worth, deliver an experience that measures up. The focus shifts from connection to conquest, from presence to performance. Many men find themselves rehearsing lines, strategizing moves, or comparing themselves to others, trapped in their heads rather than in their bodies.

Rewiring in the context of dating means stepping off the treadmill of performance and reclaiming the body as sacred. Instead of chasing approval or numbing emptiness with casual encounters, a man learns to carry himself with calm confidence, rooted not in what others think but in how deeply he feels his own vitality.

This is not about rejecting dating; it is about engaging differently. The single man who honors his body and energy approaches dates not as auditions but as opportunities for genuine resonance. He does not need to inflate his stories or exaggerate experiences because he lives in authenticity. His presence, not his performance, is what leaves a lasting impression. If dating feels like performance, pause the script. Go for short, real conversations. Say what you mean. Do not chase. Do not play cold. Protect your energy by being clear.

In this way, the rewired man brings something rare into modern dating: steadiness, clarity, and reverence. He is not frantic or needy; he is grounded. This groundedness creates a magnetic field that both attracts and filters, drawing to him partners who resonate with his energy while naturally repelling those who seek only surface-level games.

Dating then shifts from being an exhausting cycle of performance to a sacred practice of discernment, presence, and embodied truth.

2.3 Marriage & Routine

Marriage can be both sanctuary and crucible for the masculine body. It offers companionship, stability, and intimacy, but it can also create patterns that leave men disconnected from themselves. Over time, the rhythm of daily life, work, children, bills, and responsibility, can turn intimacy into obligation rather than exploration. In many marriages, routine gradually dulls presence. Sexual connection can become mechanical: a duty, a scheduled release, or something that fades into the background. This is rarely because love is gone, but because habit replaces awareness.

A man who was once attentive to his body and his partner may slowly drift into autopilot, treating sex as another box to check. Routine kills desire when attention disappears. Bring attention back. Ten minutes of presence beats two hours of distracted time.

Added to this is the silent weight of expectation. Men often feel they must perform sexually in marriage, as though intimacy is measured by endurance, frequency, or results. That pressure hollows out genuine connection, leaving both partners unsatisfied.

The deeper issue is not the loss of passion, but the loss of presence. When a man lives in his head , thinking about work, worrying about performance, distracted by stress, he robs himself and his partner of true intimacy.

Rewiring the masculine body within marriage means breaking free from routine and reclaiming the body as a living, vibrant part of union. It does not require constant novelty or performance, but awareness and sensation even within familiar rhythms. Approach each encounter with openness, curiosity, and reverence for both bodies.

When a man honors his own body, feeling fully, breathing deeply, and slowing down, he brings new energy into the marriage. Instead of obligation, intimacy becomes a shared ritual of presence. Instead of pressure, there is play. Instead of autopilot, there is embodiment.

Marriage provides fertile ground for this rewiring. Within its safety and trust, a man can relearn how to be in tune with his energy and vibration, releasing stress and stepping into calm confidence. Daily life that once dulled connection can become a practice of renewal when met with discipline, awareness, and devotion.

2.4 Second Life After Divorce

For many men, the period following divorce marks a crossroads, a time when everything that once felt stable is upended. Roles change. Family rhythms dissolve. The identity of "husband" can disappear overnight. It is no surprise this season brings feelings of loss, guilt, confusion, and at times, a hollow sense of failure. Yet second life is also a chance. Unlike youth, where much is stumbled into, or marriage, where expectations dominate, this season often demands deeper intentionality. Here a man can ask: Who am I without the titles? What does my body mean to me now? What is my worth apart from performance and provision?

In this stage, the culture of performance can weigh heavily. Men often rush back into dating, carrying the same pressure to prove, to themselves, to peers, to imagined critics. Performance becomes a test. Body image becomes a battlefield. Even solitude can feel like evidence of inadequacy.

But when approached with reverence, this stage can be profoundly liberating. No longer bound by youthful immaturity or marital routine, a man can use this time to rewrite his script: You do not need to fix your past to build your future. You need clean habits and honest boundaries. Start there.

- Body as Temple, Not Tool: Instead of using sex or attention as proof of value, rediscover the body as sacred.
- Presence Over Proving: Let intimacy shift away from conquest toward presence, being fully there in sensation, energy, and connection.
- Integration of Past Lessons: Divorce carries wounds, but also wisdom. Use it to integrate discipline, boundaries, and self-respect.

Second life after divorce is not about returning to adolescence or replaying old habits. It is about stepping into maturity with clarity, honoring the body, grounding in self-worth, and learning to experience intimacy not through anxious proving but through calm appreciation. The male body ceases to be a reminder of failure and becomes the foundation for renewed power.

> **Try This:**
>
> Notice how you hold your body when you feel desired vs. when you feel judged

Chapter 3

A GENERAL GUIDE TO MALE PLEASURE ZONES

"Curiosity is attractive"

This section is for education, not conquest. The purpose is to learn a map so you can slow down, feel more, and respect the process. Curiosity and consent guide everything. This is not a sex-education manual. It is a guide to presence, sensation, and self-respect. Whether you explore one area or none at all, the point is to understand that your body holds many pathways to awareness. What matters is curiosity without judgment and attention without shame.

To cultivate presence and move beyond performance culture, it helps to recognize that the male body contains many potential sources of sensation. Exploring these consciously builds awareness and sensitivity throughout your whole system.

Pressure, pace, and breath change everything. Lighter touch combined with slower breathing tends to heighten sensation in most areas. Check in often, notice what shifts, and adjust.

The illustration provided offers a simplified reference for the primary male pleasure zones and their relationship to energy flow, vitality, and awareness. These areas are not isolated points of stimulation; they are gateways that connect physical sensation with energetic balance and emotional presence.

General Guide to Male Pleasure Zones

A practical map of awareness, grounding, and energy flow through the male body.

Heart
Sacral
Prostate
Scrotum   Perineum   Anus / Pelvic Floor
Root / Ground

A practical map of awareness, grounding, and energy flow through the male body. These zones are not about performance, but awareness and learning to feel, regulate, and direct energy with intention.

Area	Energy / Function	Physical Benefit	Energetic Flow
Scrotum (Testicles)	Creative energy, life force	Hormonal balance, vitality	Root to Sacral center
Perineum	Grounding, root connection	Pelvic floor strength, blood flow, Circulation, Vitality	Base of energy circuit
Anus / Pelvic Floor	Release and stability	Digestion, tension release	Root-to-core grounding
Prostate	Power, deep pleasure, masculine confidence	Circulation, orgasmic health	Bridge between physical and subtle energy
Heart & Breath Overlay	Compassion, openness	Blood oxygenation, calm	Connects lower centers to higher consciousness

21

1) Scrotum (Testicles)
- Why: The seat of life force. Gentle attention here brings warmth, grounding, and a sense of vitality
- How: Use light cupping, slow rolling, or soft fingertip strokes with a little oil. Apply less pressure than you think you need. Move with breath and awareness

2) Perineum
- Why: Known as the "root gate," this area connects to key pelvic nerves and influences the flow of sexual energy
- How: Use two fingers flat with gentle, steady pressure, or small circular movements. Keep your breath deep and synchronized with touch

3) Buttocks & Anus (Pelvic Floor, Optional)
- Why: his region contains a dense network of nerves. External touch can ground awareness and heighten sensation. Reclaiming this area helps dissolve shame and tension often held in the pelvic floor.
- How: Knead the buttocks slowly. For the anus, begin only with external exploration: light fingertip circles or gentle pressure while maintaining relaxed breathing. Never rush; awareness matters more than intensity.

4) Prostate (Advanced, Optional)
- Why: Sometimes called the "male G-spot," the prostate can unlock deep waves of sensation and release when approached with patience and care.
- How: Only explore this once you feel comfortable with external touch. Use ample lubricant, proceed slowly, and focus on breath and relaxation. The goal is awakening and awareness, not speed or climax.

Recap and Perspective

The purpose of mapping these zones is awareness, not performance. You are not being told to try everything listed. These areas are simply part of the male body and acknowledging them helps remove shame and rebuild connection.

When you approach the body this way, with breath, patience, and respect, sensation becomes more than stimulation. It becomes a form of listening.

Chapter 4

PRACTICES AND RE-WIRING
(SELF-WORK)

"Ritual is repetition with respect"

Awareness is only the first step. To live differently, men must retrain body, mind, and energy. The modern male body has often been conditioned to live in performance mode: doing rather than feeling, proving rather than being. Rewiring requires practices that quiet the mind, awaken sensation, and restore presence. These are not luxuries; they are disciplines. These practices are not about performance or technique. They are frameworks for re-patterning your nervous system through breath, touch, movement, and awareness. Adapt them as you go. Comfort and curiosity matter more than completion. These practices come from my training in Tantra, Reiki, and somatic coaching. The goal is not to add noise. The goal is to reduce it.

4.1 Breath as Anchor

- Practice: Slow abdominal breathing (4–6 seconds in, 6–8 seconds out). Place one hand on your chest, one on your lower belly, ensuring the belly rises first.
- Tip: Breath for 3 minutes Inhale 4, hold 4, exhale 4, hold 4. If your mind races, count out loud. When in doubt, lengthen the exhale.
- Effect: Shifts the body out of fight-or-flight, calms the nervous system, and teaches feeling into the core rather than only the head.

4.2 Conscious Touch (Solo Practice)

Instead of chasing climax or numbing with distraction, conscious touch rewires the nervous system to feel again.
- Practice: Explore the body slowly, using varied pressure and rhythm. Avoid rushing toward release. Speak inwardly: This is my body, my vessel, my power.
- Tip: Use a timer for 5 to 10 minutes. Touch with no goal. Track sensation from 0 to 10. When it drops, change pressure or area. You are training attention.
- Effect: Re-sensitizes nerve pathways dulled by speed, porn, or routine. Cultivates appreciation and reverence rather than shame or performance.

4.3 Movement and Stillness

The male body stores tension in shoulders, hips, and pelvic floor. Without release, this tension interrupts sensation and flow.
- Practice: Alternate between dynamic movement (yoga, stretching, shaking, martial forms) and still meditation.
- Tip: Pick one pattern daily: 5 salutations, 2 minutes of shaking out energy, or even a 5 minute walk without your phone. Do it at the same time each day.
- Effect: Clears stagnant energy, improves circulation, and creates a sense of grounded openness.

4.4 Emotional Release

Release is not just physical, it's emotional and energetic. Men often suppress emotion until it becomes tension or compulsive behavior. Learning to release consciously allows energy to circulate freely again.
- Practice: Find a safe space to breathe deeply and express through sound, movement, or tears and without judgment. If emotion arises, let it move through you.
- Tip: Place a hand on your heart or belly and breathe until you feel a subtle shift or softness.
- End with stillness and gratitude for what was released.

Conscious Self-Practice (Steps)

This practice is about rewiring your relationship with your body and moving away from performance, fantasy, or quick release and toward presence, sensation, and reverence. It's not just about the penis. The entire male body is alive with zones of pleasure, and by learning to slow down and explore them without shame, you restore sensitivity and presence that will serve both solo practice and partnered intimacy.

1) Mindset & Breath

- Begin with slow abdominal breathing. Inhale deeply, let your belly rise; exhale fully and relax your shoulders.
- Set an intention: I honor my body. I am here to feel.
- Release thoughts of performance or fantasy. The practice is about noticing, not proving.

2) Penis Resensitization & Pelvic Floor Work

Glans (Head)

- Use fingertips or a lightly oiled palm to circle or gently stroke.
- Pause often, rest your hand on the glans, breathing into the sensitivity.
- Instead of rushing, let the smallest sensations come forward.

Shaft

- Stroke with slower speed and lighter pressure than usual. Experiment with variation:
- Slow glide: base to tip, steady pressure. Twist stroke: add a soft spiral motion.
- Base hold: use the other hand at the root, pressing lightly to direct awareness upward. Match strokes with breath (inhale upward, exhale downward).

3) Scrotum & Testicles

- Cup them gently in your hand, let their weight rest into your palm.
- Lightly massage or roll them, bringing blood flow and warmth.
- This both relaxes and awakens deeper sexual energy.

4) Perineum

- The space between scrotum and anus is rich with nerves.
- Use a fingertip or knuckle to press lightly or massage in circles.
- This amplifies sensation and connects external touch to internal energy flow.

5) Anus & Prostate Awareness

Not every man will feel drawn to explore this area, and there is no requirement to do so. It is included for education, not expectation
- With body-safe oil, explore light touch around the anal ring.
- Start with gentle pressure or massage, there is no rush or expectation toward penetration.
- If comfortable, gradual internal exploration can stimulate the prostate, heightening arousal and clearing deep tension.
- Approach without shame, these sensations are part of the male body's design and can deepen overall awareness.

6) Integration

- Alternate between these zones, not to reach orgasm quickly, but to circulate sensation throughout the body.
- When arousal builds, slow down. Hold yourself, breathe, and affirm: This body is powerful. I honor its sensations.

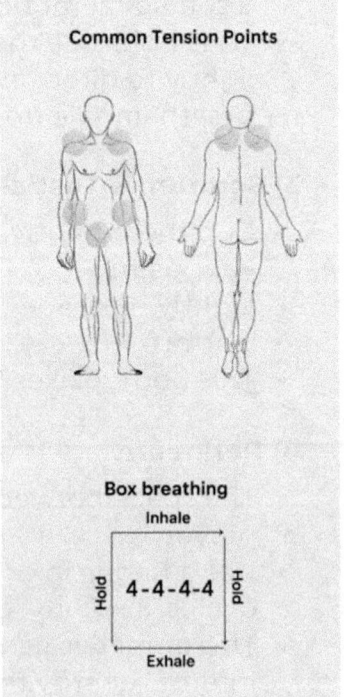

Self-Practice Checklist

- Breathe & Settle
- 5 slow abdominal breaths.
- Intention: I honor my body. I am here to feel.
- Penis Awareness
- Gentle strokes of the glans.
- Slow, varied shaft strokes (glide, twist, base hold).
- Focus on sensitivity, not speed.
- Scrotum
- Cup, massage lightly, roll gently.
- Notice warmth and weight.
- Perineum & Anus

(Continued Next Page)

Self-Practice Checklist (Continued)
- Light circular pressure on perineum.
- Optional gentle anal touch if comfortable.
- Integration & Choice
- Pause, breathe, notice full-body sensation.

Rewiring is not a weekend project. It is steady repetition, not intensity, that changes the system. The goal is not to master these techniques but to inhabit your own body with greater respect and clarity. Every breath, every touch, every pause is practice.

Chapter 5

PARTNER WORK

"Depth is built through trust and safety"

Up to this point, the focus has been on solo practices: slowing down, resensitizing, and reclaiming presence in your own body. These foundations matter because intimacy with a partner unfolds in real time, without the space for deliberate breathing exercises or ritual setups. Partner work is where your rewiring is tested, expressed, and shared.

Partner work is not advanced because it is sexual. It is advanced because it requires honesty. Agree on consent, pace, and words before you begin. If trust rises, intensity can rise. If trust drops, slow down.

Shifting From Performance to Presence
- Old script: sex framed as a performance: lasting long enough, staying hard enough, making sure she orgasms.
- New script: sex as shared presence - feeling your body, feeling hers, letting connection guide rhythm. Presence replaces pressure. When you are present, performance takes care of itself.

Translating Solo Practice Into Partnered Intimacy
- The same principles apply: slowness, sensation, and breath.
- Instead of rushing into penetration, explore touch, kissing, massage, or playful teasing. Notice how your own body feels in each moment, not just hers.
- Let your partner's responses guide pace and depth rather than mental goals.

Communication as Embodiment
- Simple words like "slower," "softer," "yes, right there" create a live feedback loop.
- Eye contact, shared breath, or synchronized movement bring both bodies into the same rhythm.
- This isn't about asking "Am I doing good?", it's about creating connection in the moment.

Expanding Pleasure Zones Together
- Exploration of these areas is optional and should only happen with mutual openness and consent.
- What you explored solo: scrotum, perineum, gentle anal touch, can also enrich partnered intimacy if there's mutual openness.
- Introducing new zones isn't about novelty for its own sake; it's about breaking free from narrow conditioning that reduces sex to penetration alone.
- When partners explore each other's full bodies, shame drops, curiosity rises, and intimacy deepens.
- From Quick Release to Shared Arc
- Solo work trains you to slow down; partner work allows you to co-create pace.
- If you feel yourself racing toward climax, pause - shift positions, breathe, or return to kissing.
- Sometimes release is right, sometimes retention heightens energy. What matters is choice, not compulsion.

The Reward of Presence
- The greatest gift you bring into intimacy is not a trick or technique, it's your embodied presence.
- When you've trained your nervous system to stay calm and feel, your partner feels it too.
- This presence builds trust, safety, and a deeper kind of desire that no performance can match.
- Partner work is not about technique. It is about translating presence into shared connection.

Guided Partner Flows

Matched Breathing

In Tantra, breath leads the moment. Match breathing for two minutes before any touch. It settles both bodies. Then start with a simple protocol Three rounds of 3 minutes.
1. Eye contact and breath.
2. Non-sexual touch, ask and adjust.
3. Sexual touch, slow, check in.

Both partners breathe *in and out together*, at the same pace and timing.

Alternate Counterpoint Breathing

One partner inhales while the other exhales. A rhythmic exchange of energy.

Penetration Presence Practice

Before: pause together, breathe, and silently affirm: I am here for sensation, not performance.
Entry: move slowly. Pay attention to every inch of penetration.
- During: focus on feeling: the glide, the pulse, the heat.
- Adjustment: shift angle, rhythm, of depth whenever needed to stay in sensation.
- Result: let go of "getting somewhere." The goal is being fully in the now.

Sensation Mapping Together

- Setup: one partner relaxes, the other explores with hands, lips, or fingertips.
- Feedback: the receiving partner gives simple cues: "More pressure." "Lighter." "Stay there."
- Switch: trade roles after a few minutes.
- Intention: builds trust and teaches both partners what truly feels good.
- Stop–Start Flow
- Notice: if climax rushes, pause while staying connected.
- Anchor: breathe and look at each other.
- Resume: begin again when the urgency softens.
- Repeat: cycle between motion and pause, letting arousal expand rather than collapse.

Stop–Start Flow
- Notice: if climax rushes, pause while staying connected.
- Anchor: breathe and look at each other.
- Resume: begin again when the urgency softens.
- Repeat: cycle between motion and pause, letting arousal expand rather than collapse.

Exploration & Openness Exchange
- Invitation: "Can I show you what I like?"
- Exchange: demonstrate your preferences, then invite your partner to share theirs.
- Zones: explore the whole body: thighs, back, chest, buttocks, scrotum, perineum, or wherever curiosity arises.
- Outcome: the body becomes a landscape of
- discovery, not a stage of performance.

Eye Contact Hold
- Pause: stop movement during intimacy. Hold eye contact for several breaths.
- Allow: feel whatever arises - closeness, vulnerability, desire.
- Continue: resume when ready, carrying that presence into the next rhythm.

Chapter 6

WHY THIS WORKS

"Attention is the lever"

Two systems explain these results. Neuroscience says interoception powers regulation. Energy work teaches that attention directs flow. Both point to the same thing. When you feel accurately, you act accurately. What you practice under no pressure is what shows up under pressure. That is why short daily reps change sex, stress, and leadership.

6.1 Rewiring Attention & Sensation (Interoception)

Most men grow up externalizing focus on performance, outcomes, others' judgments. By slowing down and practicing conscious touch, you train interoceptive pathways: the ability to feel what's happening inside your body. These attention pathways are plastic. The more you practice feeling, the more sensation you gain.

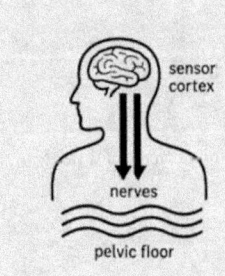

Note:
- Interoception = body awareness
- Parasympathetic = relaxation
- Practice builds new neural pathways

6.2 Resetting the Nervous System

Fast, compulsive sexual activity drives the body into a sympathetic ("fight-or-flight") state, which blunts sensation and reduces control. Slow breathing, conscious touch, and presence activate the parasympathetic ("rest-and-digest") system. This balance increases blood flow, heightens sensitivity, and allows arousal without overwhelming the system.

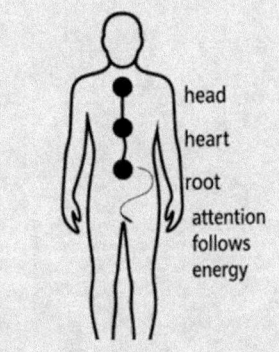

6.3 Conditioning & Re-sensitization

Pornography, distraction, and performance pressure can condition men to need constant novelty or extreme stimulation. By retraining with slower strokes, varied pressure, and sensation mapping, you desensitize old triggers while resensitizing natural touch. Excitement returns to the body, not to fantasy or visuals.

6.4 Pelvic Floor & Circulation

The pelvic floor and prostate play a central role in sexual sensation. Gentle, conscious practices strengthen awareness and circulation here, increasing arousal and control. Over time, this builds a body that can sustain sensation longer and climax with more intensity, or hold energy without release when desired.

6.5 Presence & Secure Connection

Presence is inherently magnetic. When you are not lost in your head but anchored in your body, your partner feels it. This fosters trust, reduces anxiety on both sides, and transforms intimacy into exploration instead of performance.

How Long Does It Take?

Every man is different, but a common arc looks like:
- Stage 1: initial awareness; noticing rushing or wandering; sensation begins to sharpen.
- Stage 2: early rewiring; solo practice feels natural; presence during intimacy increases; old habits still appear but are noticed sooner.
- Stage 3: control and sensitivity rise; less dependent on fantasy; partners notice calm confidence.
- Stage 4: a new baseline; presence and sensation feel natural; old performance habits no longer dominate.

This is not a rigid timeline. Progress is about consistency, not perfection. Even a few minutes a day of mindful practice can compound into lasting change.

Common Roadblocks

- Drifting into fantasy: notice, breathe, return to sensation.
- Feeling nothing at first: stay consistent; nerves resensitize over time.
- Partner hesitation: invite dialogue, reassure without pressure, focus on shared exploration.
- Busy weeks: fall back on breath and touch: maintenance beats intensity.

The Core Principle

Energy follows attention. When you redirect attention inward, slow down, and honor your body, your nervous system, muscles, and arousal patterns adapt. You stop being ruled by performance scripts and instead embody presence, sensation, and calm confidence

Integration

Science explains the how around attention, nerves, muscles, conditioning. Beneath the physiology, the deeper truth remains: presence and energy are sacred. Every practice here is not just a technique but a way of honoring the body as a vessel of life force. When you slow down, feel fully, and release old patterns of performance, you do more than rewire your brain, you reclaim your worth. This work restores your body as a temple and your presence as a gift.

Rewiring is not about becoming someone new. It is about remembering the version of you that could feel fully, act clearly, and love without performance.

Chapter 7

THE QUICK START GUIDE

"Start small. Stay honest. The body will remember what the mind forgets."

Awareness means little without consistent action. The practices in Chapter 5 were designed to reconnect body, mind, and energy, but the real shift happens through rhythm and repetition. This Quick Start Guide offers a simple structure for integrating the work into daily life. It's not about doing everything. It's about doing one thing well and consistently enough for your nervous system, emotions, and habits to begin re-patterning.

7.1 The Framework

One practice. One line. One real talk. Every 14 days, review and evolve. These 4 pillars are your foundation for embodied change. They keep the process grounded, measurable, and alive.

① **One Practice**
Choose one daily anchor from Chapter 5.

② **One Line**
Journal a single line after each practice.

③ **One Talk**
Share one honest reflection weekly.

④ **14-Day Review**
Reflect, adjust, and evolve every two weeks.

REPEAT → REVIEW → ADJUST →

7.2 Step 1 - Choose One Daily Practice

From Chapter 5, select one of the following:
- Breath as Anchor.
- Conscious Touch (Solo Practice).
- Movement and Stillness.
- Emotional Release.

How to Begin
- Commit to the same time each day (morning, mid-day, or evening).
- Keep it short - 5 to 10 minutes.
- Let the intention be presence, not performance. As an example: 5 minutes of slow abdominal breathing each morning before coffee, or 2 minutes of shaking out energy followed by stillness before bed.

Why it matters:
- Repetition rewires the nervous system. The time of day doesn't matter: the consistency does.

7.3 Step 2 - Journal One Line

After each daily practice, record a single sentence. Use three simple prompts:
- Sensation: What did I feel?
- Thought: What came to mind?
- Action: What do I need or want now?
- Example: "Tight shoulders, breath deepened, felt calmer." or "Calming in chest, gratitude, texted my brother."

Why it matters:
- This connects awareness (feeling) to cognition (thought) and behavior (action).
- Over time, it strengthens self-trust and emotional clarity.

7.4 Step 3 - One Honest Talk Per Week

Once a week, have a short, real check-in with a trusted person such as a partner, friend, or mentor.
- Keep it simple:
- "Here's what I practiced."
- "Here's what I noticed."
- "Here's what changed."

Why it matters:
Speaking truth out loud reinforces authenticity. It transforms inner work into relational integrity and creating a bridge between healing and connection.

7.5 Step 4 - Review Every 14 Days

At the end of each two-week cycle:
- Reread your journal entries.
- Notice patterns.
- Ask what's working, what isn't, and what needs adjusting.

Then decide:
- Continue the same practice if it's deepening your awareness.
- Shift to another if you feel stagnant.

Why it matters:
- Reflection keeps your growth intentional and adaptive.
- You're training evolution, not perfection itself.

7.6 The Spirit of the Practice

This is not a challenge. It's a rhythm, a conversation between your body, breath, and awareness.
- If you miss a day, return the next.
- If you feel numb, stay curious.
- If you feel resistance, meet it with breath.

Over time, the practices that begin as effort become natural expressions of who you are.

Consistency is the bridge between awareness and embodiment.

Chapter 8
CLOSING REFLECTIONS

This work has asked you to slow down, to step out of old scripts, and to meet yourself in a new way. It is not about chasing perfection, but about reclaiming presence in your body, in your breath, and in every moment you give or receive touch. The Divine Masculine is not performance, conquest, or output. It is calm strength, steady energy, and the courage to feel fully.

The practices you've explored, whether in solitude or with a partner, are not meant to be finished like a checklist. They are invitations to return to sensation, to honor your body as sacred, and to recognize your body as sacred, to recognize that what you bring into intimacy is more than arousal, it is your presence, your energy, your wholeness.

Core Take-Away's:
- Presence is Power
- Feeling is leadership
- Sacred does not mean soft.

You have seen how early conditioning, cultural pressures, and habits of performance can dull sensation and distract you from the very experience you crave. You've also seen that with patience and discipline, the body can be rewired. Breath by breath, touch by touch, moment by moment, you can rediscover your body as a source of clarity, vitality, and worth.

To the man who practices: you are not broken. You are not behind. You are on the path. Every pause to feel your breath, every moment you slow down to listen to your body, every time you choose presence over performance, you are reclaiming something sacred.

And to the partner who walks alongside: your openness and curiosity matter. Intimacy is not one-sided. When presence meets presence, both are nourished. When trust is cultivated, both can surrender. When bodies are honored, both can be free. This is the embodiment of the Divine Masculine and Feminine working in harmony.

This journey does not end here. The pages close, but the practice remains. The invitation is to keep meeting yourself, at night when you lie in stillness, in the morning as you breathe into your chest, in the moments of intimacy where you remember to feel rather than think. Over time, these practices become less of an exercise and more of who you are: a man embodied, alive, grounded, and unashamed of his power.

You do not have to wait to feel ready. Pick one practice, run it for 30 days, and write one honest line per day. Let results stack. Let your body teach you.

Let this closing be an opening into a life where you do not perform your masculinity but inhabit it. Where your body is no longer reduced to utility, but recognized as a vessel of presence, strength, and sacred energy.

The Divine Masculine Body is not a body to be hidden, dulled, or shamed. It is a body to be lived in, fully.

www.ingramcontent.com/pod-product-compliance
Lightning Source LLC
LaVergne TN
LVHW051206080426
835508LV00021B/2834